KITCHENER PUBLIC LIBRARY

W9-DGH-218

6/09

-2

Counting by: Threes

Esther Sarfatti

Rourke
Publishing LLC
Vero Beach, Florida 32964

© 2008 Rourke Publishing LLC

All rights reserved. No part of this book may be reproduced or utilized in any form or by any means, electronic or mechanical including photocopying, recording, or by any information storage and retrieval system without permission in writing from the publisher.

www.rourkepublishing.com

PHOTO CREDITS: © Eileen Hart: title page and pages 5 and 21; © Jean Frooms: page 3; © James Steidl: page 7; © Christine Balderas: page 9; © Ramona Heim: page 11; © Jason Lugo: page 13; © Michael Ledray: page 19; © Terry Reimink: page 23.

Editor: Robert Stengard-Olliges

Cover design by Nicola Stratford.

Library of Congress Cataloging-in-Publication Data

Sarfatti, Esther.
  Counting by : threes / Esther Sarfatti.
     p. cm. -- (Concepts)
  ISBN 978-1-60044-523-1 (Hardcover)
  ISBN 978-1-60044-664-1 (Softcover)
  1. Counting--Juvenile literature. I. Title.
   QA113.S3563 2008
   513.2'11--dc22
                                    2007014071

Printed in the USA

CG/CG

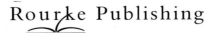

Rourke Publishing

www.rourkepublishing.com – rourke@rourkepublishing.com
Post Office Box 3328, Vero Beach, FL 32964

This is three.

What comes in threes?

A traffic light has three lights.

7

A tricycle has three wheels.

A triangle has three sides.

11

This flag has three colors.

This clownfish has three stripes.

This sundae has three scoops.

This lizard has three horns.

18

This family has three kids.

These three kids are triplets.
Counting by threes is fun!

Index

Further Reading

Fitzkee, Jeremy. *One, Two, Three, Me.* Viking Penguin, 2006.
Jacobson, David. *Three Wishes.* Sterling, 2006.

Recommended Websites

www.edhelper.com/kindergarten/Number_3.htm
www.enchantedlearning.com/languagebooks/spanish/numbers/

About the Author

Esther Sarfatti has worked with children's books for over 15 years as an editor and translator. This is her first series as an author. Born in Brooklyn, New York, and brought up in a trilingual home, Esther currently lives with her husband and son in Madrid, Spain.

Visual Geography Series®

BRAZIL

...in Pictures

Prepared by
Nathan A. Haverstock

Lerner Publications Company
Minneapolis

REMOVED
FROM
COLLECTION

WEST ISLIP PUBLIC LIBRARY
3 HIGBIE LANE
WEST ISLIP, NEW YORK 11795

Copyright © 1987 by Lerner Publications Company

All rights reserved. International copyright secured. No part of this book may be reproduced, stored in a retrieval system, or transmitted in any form or by any means—electronic, mechanical, photocopying, recording, or otherwise—without the prior written permission of the publisher, except for the inclusion of brief quotations in an acknowledged review.

Courtesy of United Nations

A sailboat makes its way up the São Francisco River near Catinga.

This is an all-new edition of the Visual Geography Series. Previous editions have been published by Sterling Publishing Company, New York City, and some of the original textual information has been retained. New photographs, maps, charts, captions, and updated information have been added. The text has been entirely reset in 10/12 Century Textbook.

LIBRARY OF CONGRESS CATALOGING-IN-PUBLICATION DATA

Haverstock, Nathan A.
  Brazil in pictures.

  (Visual geography series)
  Rev. ed. of: Brazil in pictures / prepared by
E. W. Egan.
  Includes index.
  Summary: Text and illustrations describe the history, geography, politics, and society of South America's largest country.
  1. Brazil—Juvenile literature. [1. Brazil]
I. Egan, E. W. Brazil in pictures. II. Title.
III. Series: Visual geography series (Minneapolis, Minn.)
F2508.5.H38 1987   981   86-15368
ISBN 0-8225-1802-3 (lib. bdg.)

International Standard Book Number: 0-8225-1802-3
Library of Congress Catalog Card Number: 86-15368

VISUAL GEOGRAPHY SERIES®

Publisher
Harry Jonas Lerner
Associate Publisher
Nancy M. Campbell
Executive Series Editor
Lawrence J. Zwier
Assistant Series Editor
Mary M. Rodgers
Editorial Assistant
Nora W. Kniskern
Illustrations Editor
Nathan A. Haverstock
Consultants/Contributors
Dr. Ruth F. Hale
Nathan A. Haverstock
Sandra K. Davis
Designer
Jim Simondet
Cartographer
Carol F. Barrett
Indexer
Kristine S. Schubert
Production Manager
Richard J. Hannah

Courtesy of United Nations

Favela de Rocinha, a slum area, is part of Rio de Janeiro.

Acknowledgments

Title page photo by Mary L. Daniel.

Elevation contours adapted from *The Times Atlas of the World*, seventh comprehensive edition (New York: Times Books, 1985).

Courtesy of United Nations
With what seems to be a big job ahead, a young woman draws out strands of sisal to be bundled at a plant near Petrolina in northeastern Brazil.

Contents

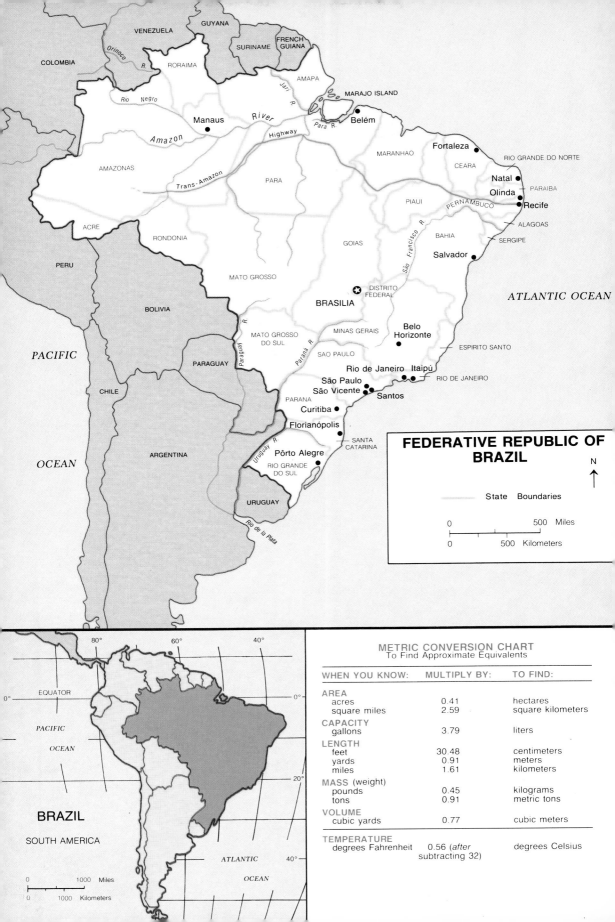

FEDERATIVE REPUBLIC OF BRAZIL

N
↑

State Boundaries

0 ——— 500 Miles

0 ——— 500 Kilometers

VENEZUELA
GUYANA
SURINAME
FRENCH GUIANA
COLOMBIA
Orinoco R.
RORAIMA
AMAPA
MARAJO ISLAND
Rio Negro
Jari R.
Amazon River
Manaus
Highway
Belém
MARANHAO
Fortaleza
Para R.
CEARA
RIO GRANDE DO NORTE
AMAZONAS
Trans-Amazon
PARA
Natal
PARAIBA
Olinda
PERNAMBUCO
Recife
PIAUI
ACRE
São Francisco R.
ALAGOAS
RONDONIA
BAHIA
SERGIPE
GOIAS
Salvador
PERU
MATO GROSSO
ATLANTIC OCEAN
BOLIVIA
BRASILIA
DISTRITO FEDERAL
Paraguay R.
MATO GROSSO DO SUL
MINAS GERAIS
Belo Horizonte
Parana R.
SAO PAULO
ESPIRITO SANTO
PARAGUAY
Rio de Janeiro
Itaipú
PACIFIC
São Paulo
RIO DE JANEIRO
CHILE
São Vicente
Santos
PARANA
Curitiba
OCEAN
Florianópolis
Uruguay R.
SANTA CATARINA
Pôrto Alegre
ARGENTINA
RIO GRANDE DO SUL
URUGUAY
Rio de la Plata

BRAZIL

SOUTH AMERICA

EQUATOR
0°
80°
60°
40°
PACIFIC
OCEAN
20°
ATLANTIC
OCEAN
40°

0 ——— 1000 Miles
0 ——— 1000 Kilometers

METRIC CONVERSION CHART
To Find Approximate Equivalents

WHEN YOU KNOW:	MULTIPLY BY:	TO FIND:
AREA		
acres	0.41	hectares
square miles	2.59	square kilometers
CAPACITY		
gallons	3.79	liters
LENGTH		
feet	30.48	centimeters
yards	0.91	meters
miles	1.61	kilometers
MASS (weight)		
pounds	0.45	kilograms
tons	0.91	metric tons
VOLUME		
cubic yards	0.77	cubic meters
TEMPERATURE		
degrees Fahrenheit	0.56 (*after* subtracting 32)	degrees Celsius

Courtesy of David Mangurian

Brazilian optimism is reflected in the enthusiastic thumbs-up sign given by a gaucho of southern Brazil. A surging economy and the revival of civilian rule have instilled the citizens of the largest country in South America with a sense of great possibilities.

Introduction

A teacher at a junior high school in Kansas, her class enlarged one day by half a dozen Latin American visitors, carefully drew a map of South America on the blackboard. When she had finished and had lettered in the names of the countries, her map was of the right shape, but one country was missing: Brazil. One of the visitors, a Brazilian, approached the teacher after class and, in his imperfect English, pointed out the omission. The teacher was embarrassed at having left South America's largest country off her map, but she and the Brazilian had a good laugh about it. "I wouldn't have thought it possible to

draw a map of South America without Brazil," the visitor said later to a friend.

The teacher's mistake was possible in the United States because Brazil gets so little attention in the schools. The language of Brazil, Portuguese, is taught at few—if any—U.S. public schools below the university level, even though it is the language of half of South America's people. By contrast, Spanish is taught at most U.S. public schools.

When Brazil is discussed in classrooms at all, it is usually lumped together with some three dozen other countries in Latin America and the Caribbean with which it

has little in common historically, culturally, or economically. Its most talked-about feature, the sparsely populated (though huge) Amazon Basin, is an area that most Brazilians have never visited.

Little time is devoted to discussing modern, progressive Brazil. The largest Brazilian city, industrial São Paulo, has more than 30,000 factories and a metropolitan population (which combines the number of actual city dwellers with those who live in outlying, suburban areas) of 12.5 million. From 1970 to 1980, São Paulo added 23,000 streets to accommodate the 3.5 million vehicles—most of them Brazilian-made—that entered its stream of traffic.

Bountiful natural resources and the hard work of its people are the foundations of Brazil's emergence as a world power. In 1985, Brazil's economic growth rate was higher than that of any other major nation. Twenty years ago, Brazil had to import food from the United States; now the fertile farmlands of southern Brazil—

Courtesy of United Nations

A forestry expert measures the girth of a tree in Brazil's Amazon jungle, a living resource that influences worldwide climate.

South America's breadbasket—produce food that is being exported to help feed the hungry of Africa.

Problems remain, however. Traditional old Brazil in the northeast, where plantations of cotton and sugar were once worked by black slaves from Africa, has been left far behind in the nation's industrialization. The northeast suffers from widespread poverty as a result. Also, uncertainty surrounds Brazil's efforts to make the vast Amazon Basin productive; taming the rain-forests could upset global ecological systems.

But Brazilians are confident. Recent advances have instilled an already optimistic people with a sense of great possibilities. In 1985, after 20 years of military rule, Brazil took an important step in its controlled return to democracy by electing a civilian president. Brazilians see great things ahead as the drive toward full democracy continues.

Courtesy of VARIG Airlines

Brazil's presidential residence, the Alvorada Palace, is in Brasília, the capital city built from scratch in the 1950s.

Independent Picture Service

The Christ of Corcovado looks out over the white cityscape of Rio de Janeiro, toward the abrupt peak of Sugar Loaf and the irregular contours of Guanabara Bay.

1) The Land

The Federative Republic of Brazil, which has a total area of 3,286,487 square miles, is the fifth largest country in the world, after the Soviet Union, the People's Republic of China, Canada, and the United States. However, Brazil is larger than the continental United States minus Alaska.

Boundaries

Brazil encompasses nearly half the territory of the South American continent. To the north, Brazil's sparsely populated Guiana Highlands and Amazon Basin border on French Guiana (a colony), Suriname (a former Dutch colony), Guyana (a former British colony), and Venezuela. To the west, trackless Amazonian jungles form the frontier with Colombia, Peru, and Bolivia. To the southwest and south, level and productive farms and cattle lands border on Paraguay, Argentina, and Uruguay. The only South American countries with which Brazil does not share a border are Ecuador and Chile.

Topography

Topographically, Brazil is divided into three principal areas, the south, the northeast, and the Amazon Basin. These areas are so different in climate, standard of living, and resources as to constitute three nations within a nation.

7

The southern third of the nation, from north of Brasília to the Uruguayan border, is the most populous, most agriculturally developed, and most industrially modern part of the country. This area extends about 1,500 miles from north to south and about 1,000 miles from east to west at its widest. It is the location of most of Brazil's major cities—including the industrial cities of São Paulo and Belo Horizonte, the financial and tourist center of Rio de Janeiro, and the national capital of Brasília. Important secondary cities that are regional centers for commerce include Curitiba (a coffee-trading center south of São Paulo), Florianópolis, and Pôrto Alegre—the latter two in Brazil's southern breadbasket.

Much of this highly progressive region is on the central and southern plateaus, with rolling terrain at a mean elevation of some 3,000 feet. The wealth of this region has long derived from the land and the sprawling coffee plantations (*fazendas*) that up until about 25 years ago produced two-thirds of Brazil's export earnings. Toward the south, the plateaus give way to the rolling, then level, lands of Brazil's temperate zone, an area of productive farms and efficient cattle-raising operations.

Brazil's second country within a country is the northeast. This area, consisting of nine states, is twice the size of Texas and forms the hump that protrudes from South America into the Atlantic Ocean

Courtesy of David Mangurian

Florianópolis is the capital of Santa Catarina, a prosperous farming state on the Atlantic coast of southern Brazil.

The lushness of the Amazon's vegetation is apparent in an aerial view of the Gurupi River, which cuts through the Amazon rain-forest. The Gurupi forms the border between the states of Pará and Maranhão.

Photo by Mary L. Daniel

toward Africa—to which many geologists say Brazil was once physically joined. Along the coast, like buttons on the vest of a fat man, are several port cities—among them Natal, Recife (also called Pernambuco), and Salvador (also known as Bahia)—through which flow the cacao, cotton, and sugarcane grown on a narrow but fertile coastal strip.

Inland, the northeast opens onto an immense and generally level plateau where millions of subsistence farmers barely wrest a living from often drought-stricken lands in a harsh and quirky climate. In all, Brazil's northeast is home to approximately one-third of the nation's total population, the vast majority of whom are poor. The thin wrists and gaunt faces of adults, the results of their malnutrition as children in overcrowded homes, mark them for life as northeasterners, no matter where they eventually choose to live.

The third area, Amazonian Brazil, comprises half of the national territory. This is the world's largest tropical rain-forest, where 100 varieties of trees may grow on a single acre. For centuries, the tropical lowlands of the Amazon Basin have been home to scattered Indian groups. A few settlements by non-Indians were eventually established and then grew or were abandoned depending on the market value of one tropical resource or another. Today, the Amazon region has cities of its own, and the primitive cultures still surviving there are increasingly affected by outside forces associated with Brazil's national development.

Rivers: the Amazon and São Francisco

The Amazon River and its more than 1,000 tributaries—many of them sizable rivers in their own right—drain the Amazon Basin. From its source high in the Peruvian Andes, the Amazon flows for nearly 4,000 miles before emptying into the

Courtesy of United Nations

South Atlantic north of Marajó Island. It carries more water than any other river in the world and is second in length only to the Nile River.

The river is navigable for roughly half its length—as far inland as Iquitos, Peru— by oceangoing ships, which call at port cities along the way. One of these is Belém (also called Pará), which is near the mouth of the Amazon just south of the island of Marajó. About 1,000 miles inland, near the confluence of the Amazon and the Río Negro, lies another port, Manaus.

The Río Negro, which flows into the Amazon from the northwest, is also large and partially navigable. A plan has been proposed to one day link the Río Negro and the Orinoco—a river that flows north through Venezuela and empties into the Atlantic Ocean south of Trinidad—in one huge inland waterway. If these rivers were joined via canals, northern South America would have a commercial waterway of more than 4,000 miles in length—twice the length of the Mississippi River.

Brazil's second most important river is the São Francisco, which rises in the highlands of Minas Gerais state, midway between Brasília and Rio de Janeiro. It flows northward through much of Brazil's northeast before turning sharply east to empty into the Atlantic Ocean halfway between the port cities of Recife and Salvador—a distance of nearly 2,000 miles. The São Francisco is navigable for more than 1,200 miles and serves as an inland commercial artery linking northeastern and southern Brazil. The São Francisco drains an enormous area, provides water for irrigation to farms in its broad valley, and turns the turbines of huge hydroelectric installations that supply electricity to towns and cities along its course.

Southern Brazil is drained by the Río de la Plata (River Plate) system. This system includes the Paraguay River, which rises in northern Mato Grosso state; the Uruguay, which forms most of Brazil's border with Argentina; and the Paraná, which rises north of Rio de Janeiro—not far from the source of the São Francisco River— and flows across the Paraguay border. There the Paraná joins the Paraguay River, which heads south to meet the Río de la Plata, a saltwater estuary that opens onto the Atlantic Ocean. The Paraná-Paraguay Basin is South America's second largest, after the Amazon. It drains a huge southern portion of the continent, including sizable areas of Brazil and its neighbors.

Cities

Most of Brazil's cities are located in the southern half of the country. They include São Paulo, whose metropolitan population

Brazilian riverbanks are home to the capybara, which grows to a length of about four feet and is the world's largest rodent. A semi-aquatic creature with webbed feet, it moves more swiftly through the water than over land.

Independent Picture Service

of 12.5 million makes it Brazil's largest city; Rio de Janeiro, which with 9 million people has three times the population of Los Angeles; and Pôrto Alegre, which has 2.2 million people—larger than the population of Dallas. Other large cities of this area are Belo Horizonte (2.5 million), capital of a mineral-rich state; Curitiba (1.5 million), a regional industrial center and hub of the coffee trade; and Santos (400,000), the port serving São Paulo. The population of Brasília, which (in terms of north and south) is near the center of Brazil, has grown to about 450,000 since the city became the new national capital in 1960. Brasília has little industry, and the government is its major employer.

The large cities of northeast Brazil are located on the coast, where they serve as ports, state capitals, and economic and cultural centers. Chief among these cities are Recife (2.4 million), Salvador (1.8 million), and Fortaleza, also called Ceará (1.6 million).

The two major cities of Amazonian Brazil are both ports: Belém (1 million) and Manaus (650,000).

Climate

Because Brazil covers such a wide range of latitude—from about 4 degrees north of the equator to about 32 degrees south—it has a wide variety of climates. Temperate-zone Brazil (from São Paulo south) enjoys a moderate subtropical climate and seasonal changes much like those of the southeastern United States. Summers are warm to hot, with average temperatures from about 70° to about 85° F, and winters are cool, with average temperatures less than 60° F. Rain falls throughout the year but amounts to less than 40 inches.

The plateaus of central and northeast Brazil are generally hot, with daytime temperatures from 75° to 85° F except where altitude makes for cooler temperatures. Being in the tropics, this area experiences little seasonal change in temperature but does have a rainy season and a dry season. Annual rainfall varies quite a bit in this region. Some areas get as much as 60 to 80 inches of rain a year, most of it falling from December to April. Other areas, such as the highlands west of Recife, get as little as 10 to 20 inches.

11

The level lands of southern Brazil are carefully cultivated and have become a South American breadbasket. Major grain crops such as wheat and corn thrive in the temperate climate of this area.

Courtesy of Embassy of Brazil, Washington, D.C.

Courtesy of Embassy of Brazil, Washington, D.C.

Jaguars are the largest, most powerful wild cats of the Western Hemisphere. They hunt mainly at night, eating almost anything—including deer, fish, wild pigs, tapirs, turtles, and capybaras.

The Amazon Basin receives heavy rainfall all year long, more than 80 inches annually, and has midday temperatures generally in excess of 80° F. These hot, humid conditions also prevail along Brazil's Atlantic coast, where several of the country's most important cities, such as Rio de Janeiro and Recife, are located. Fortunately, ocean breezes often alleviate the heat.

The tropics of the Amazon and most coastal areas of Brazil can be pleasant to live in, provided some accommodation with climate is made. Sudden and frequent downpours mitigate the heat and freshen the environment. To take advantage of the hours during which the weather is best, Brazilians living in the tropics generally rise early—before sunrise—to work until about 10 o'clock in the morning. After lunch and a nap that lasts until about 2 o'clock in the afternoon, they work a second shift until 7 or 8 o'clock in the evening. By following this regimen, Brazilians of

13

Independent Picture Service

Royal water lilies (*Victoria amazonia*) float on the glassy surface of a tributary of the Amazon River. These wonders of the plant world may reach 10 feet in breadth and are strong enough to support the weight of a person.

Rectangular Santos-Dumont Airport juts into the sea from downtown Rio de Janeiro. Used mainly for shuttle flights between Rio and São Paulo, this field offers convenience to the business district but would create a noise problem if it were expanded to handle international jetliners. International flights use Rio International Airport on Governador Island, about 26 miles from the center of the city.

Courtesy of United Nations

the tropics enjoy what amounts to two days each single day and are awake and at work when their climate is most refreshing.

Flora and Fauna

The profuse vegetation of Brazil's Amazon Basin plays an important role in sustaining the earth's ecological balance. Because the region is so vast and because almost all of it is covered with green plants, an enormous amount of photosynthesis (the ability of green plants to convert sunlight and carbon dioxide to carbohydrates) occurs there. Without the Amazon jungles to consume carbon dioxide and release oxygen, the amounts of these gases in the earth's atmosphere might change, dramatically affecting weather patterns over the entire planet. Brazil's vegetation is, in a very real sense, a resource valuable to the whole world.

The plant life of the Amazon is remarkable for its variety as well as its quantity. Scientists have identified more than 3,000 species within a single square mile. With so great a range of plant life, the tropical forests could contain species beneficial to human beings. Some employees of international pharmaceutical companies spend their entire careers exploring the jungles for plants that might prove useful in treating disease.

The trees in the Amazon's tropical rain-forests can grow 200 feet high, and their interlocking branches can keep most of the sun's rays from reaching the forest floor. Some rain-forests, therefore, have thin ground-level vegetation. Heavy rainfalls in these areas carry away valuable soil nutrients.

Animals live at different heights beneath the forest canopy. High up, monkeys of many kinds—such as black howlers, spider monkeys, woolly monkeys, and marmosets—play in the branches. The coati, a relative of the raccoon but with a longer tail and snout, lives somewhat lower in the trees, as does the two-toed sloth, a curiously human-looking mammal that makes its way upside down along tree branches as it feeds on leaves. Several members of the cat family, notably jaguars and ocelots, prowl the forest floor.

Among the stranger creatures of Brazil is the capybara. The world's largest rodent (adults are about four feet long and weigh more than 100 pounds), it has slightly webbed feet that make it somewhat slow on land but agile in the rivers and lakes near which it lives. The tapir, South America's largest mammal, appears piglike because of its bulk but is related to the horse and rhinoceros. With its distinctive flexible snout it sniffs out the fruits and leaves on which it feeds.

Courtesy of United Nations

Brazil is one of the world's leading suppliers of mica, a crystalline mineral that breaks easily into sheets. Mica, which can contain various elements such as aluminum, silicon, and lithium, is used for protecting electrical components and for preventing and stopping fires.

Photo by Meg and Don Malde Arnosti

A bright-plumed toucan feeds on palm fruits from a perch in the Iguaçu Falls.

Among Brazil's many species of birds are some with extraordinary plumage: the big-beaked toucan; the jabiru, a kind of stork; hummingbirds of many types and colors; the scarlet ibis; and the parakeet. Another bird, the brown-crested hoatzin, gives off such a foul smell that it has been nicknamed the stinkbird.

The Amazon River itself is home to a species of freshwater dolphin and the huge manatee, also called the sea cow, which feeds voraciously on vegetable matter and thus helps to clean out rivers choked by greenery. Reptiles, including vicious caimans and alligators, abound. Within the rivers lurk fish of prehistoric appearance, game fish, and the fierce, man-eating piranha. Schools of piranha can reduce the

carcass of an animal to a skeleton within seconds, churning up the water as they devour its flesh.

Minerals

Already known to have a staggering array of mineral deposits, Brazil frequently discovers new ones. Brazil's iron ore deposits are ranked as the world's second largest, and it has abundant bauxite and manganese. In recent years, mining activity has focused on the fabulous mineral resources of a 35,000-square-mile region in the states of Pará and Maranhão in the eastern Amazon Basin. The minerals being exploited in the initial phase of this region's development have a value estimated at more than

$500 billion. They include 18 billion tons of iron ore, 60 million of manganese, and huge quantities of bauxite, nickel, tin, and gold.

The only resources in short supply are petroleum and natural gas. Despite determined exploration by Brazilian and foreign-owned companies, Brazil's proven oil reserves amount to only about two billion barrels. (Venezuela, for comparison, has proven oil reserves of about 17 billion barrels.)

To reduce its dependence on foreign petroleum, Brazil has turned to a plentiful domestic resource: sugarcane. Alcohol produced from sugar is mixed with gasoline to fuel many motor vehicles, and other Brazilian-made cars and trucks run on alcohol alone. Brazil has also constructed a long pipeline from the industrial state of São Paulo to Bolivia in order to transport natural gas from the Bolivian province of Santa Cruz.

Courtesy of Whitney Museum of New York

The lushness of Brazil's tropics inspired U.S. artist Martin J. Heade to paint *Orchids, Passion Flowers, and Hummingbirds* around 1865.

At Cristalina, near the capital city of Brasília, lies one of the world's largest quartz crystal deposits.

Photo by Mary L. Daniel

17

Brazil's Amazon Basin is an enormous treasure house of mineral wealth. At a recently improved river port, a West German vessel takes on a load of bauxite mined in the state of Pará.

Courtesy of World Bank

Courtesy of Inter-American Development Bank

To reduce its dependence on foreign oil, Brazil has developed a program to burn alcohol (made from sugarcane) instead of gasoline in cars and trucks. The legend on the government vehicle says, "powered by alcohol."

Independent Picture Sevice

In a timeless ritual predating the arrival of the Europeans, unmarried Indian men — wearing feathery leggings — line up to challenge their married brothers to wrestle.

2) History and Government

Brazil's original inhabitants lived in the area centuries before the arrival of European explorers and colonizers. The Arawaks and the Caribs lived in the north, and the Tupi-Guaranians inhabited the east. The Ge resided in the south, and the Pano spent their time in the west. Hunting in the thick forests and fishing along the coasts or in the plentiful rivers provided these peoples with their livelihoods. Some groups also gathered wild fruits that grew well in Brazil's hot climate, and others of a more settled character cultivated crops, such as cassava, a fleshy root that they used in a variety of foods.

Villages existed in the form of small clusters of long, thatched houses, which were shared by more than one family. These early Brazilian residents, who numbered from one to five million, lived a Stone Age existence, so-called because their tools and weapons were made of rock. Nevertheless, they were also gifted craftspeople and fashioned baskets, pottery, and jewelry from local materials.

Discovery and Early Settlement

Meanwhile in Europe, the age of exploration had begun in earnest in the fifteenth

Courtesy of Embassy of Brazil, Washington, D.C.

In a painting by Pedro Peres, Pedro Alvares Cabral and his crew are depicted raising a large cross in thanksgiving. Blown off course en route to India, Cabral's expedition landed in what is now the state of Bahia.

century. Navigators, backed by the wealth of powerful trading nations, went in search of direct routes to Asia, where valuable markets existed.

Unknown to the groups native to Brazil, Christopher Columbus landed in the New World in 1492, an area he mistook for Asia, or the East Indies. (It was in this way that the local inhabitants were dubbed Indians by the Europeans.) The explorer's discovery touched off a rivalry between Spain and Portugal to own the new lands. To head off a war between these two Catholic countries, Pope Alexander VI in 1493 drew a north-south Line of Demarcation about 300 miles west of the Cape Verde Islands in the Atlantic Ocean. All new ter-

ritories west of the line would be Spain's and those east of the line would be Portugal's. Both countries agreed, but then Portugal grew dissatisfied and pressed for a different line about 800 miles further west. This second demarcation, agreed to by Spain in 1494 and approved by Pope Julius II in 1506, was the legal basis for Portugal's claim to eastern Brazil—once the territory had been discovered and explored.

That discovery came in 1500, when Pedro Alvares Cabral, a Portuguese captain, was blown off course while en route to India around southern Africa. He arrived on the Brazilian coast at a point in the present-day state of Bahia and claimed the new

land for Portugal. That same year, Vicente Yáñez Pinzón of Spain explored Brazil's north coast and discovered the mouth of the Amazon River.

In 1534 King João III of Portugal initiated a system of royal land grants, thereby establishing 15 administrative units, called captaincies, within the territory of Brazil. Successful settlements grew at Olinda (near Recife) and Salvador in northeast Brazil and at São Vicente (near the port of Santos) in southern Brazil. In 1548 all the captaincies were united under the rule of an appointed governor-general, who established a new capital at Salvador.

The occupation of northern areas of Brazil by forces of the Dutch West India Company interrupted Portuguese rule over the territory. The Dutch captured Pernambuco and Olinda in 1630 and controlled the region between Maranhão Island and the lower São Francisco River. With military support from mainland Portugal, however, the colonial forces were able to regain authority in 1654. The Dutch formally renounced their Brazilian claims in 1661.

The early colonists in the northeast worked hard to establish sugarcane plantations along the coast. They enslaved the Indians to satisfy the need for a large labor force. Huge numbers of Brazil's original residents died of diseases imported by the Europeans or were killed while resisting enslavement. To replace the Indians, the colonists imported ever-increasing numbers of black slaves from Africa.

The plantations produced substantial wealth for their masters. During the latter half of the sixteenth century and the

In 1500 the Spaniard Vicente Yáñez Pinzón discovered the delta region of the Amazon, but exploration of the huge river system did not begin in earnest until about 1540.

Photo by Mary L. Daniel

entire seventeenth, the captaincies of Bahia (with its capital at Salvador) and Pernambuco (with its capital at Recife) were the prime suppliers of sugar to world markets. With additional profits from cotton and cacao (from which chocolate is made), Salvador and Recife became prominent commercial centers. Drawing on their proximity to Africa, they also became centers for the world trade in slaves.

Expansion in Southern Brazil

Early settlements in southern Brazil followed the pattern established in the northeast. But the south's great variety of natural resources eventually brought about a different kind of colonial development. For example, after gold was discovered in the area of Minas Gerais in the late seventeenth century, settlers migrated there in great numbers. These newcomers did not establish plantations, rather they set up shops and small farms that would provide goods and services to the prospectors and other new residents. Unlike Spain, whose governmental agents controlled the colonial mining industry, Portugal left such matters to independent businesspeople. These developers included people from northeast Brazil, whose sugar-based economy was faltering because their crop was unable to compete in world markets with sugar grown more cheaply in the West Indies.

The independent and reckless spirit proved particularly strong among the Portuguese and other European colonizers in what is now the state of São Paulo. During the seventeenth century, these people —often thousands at a time—banded together into armed expeditions called *bandeiras* and set off for the Brazilian interior.

Initially, these groups traveled through the forests looking for Indians, whom they sold as slaves. Later, however, the bandeiras were formed to discover or extract minerals such as gold or diamonds. Since such work often kept them in the field for several years at a stretch, the bandeiras built numerous new towns and villages, thereby extending Portuguese rule well beyond the Line of Demarcation. In the

Gauchos of southern Brazil break a spirited horse. The independent lifestyle of these cattlemen can be traced to the *bandeirantes* who pushed Brazil's frontiers ever farther in their search for minerals and cropland.

Independent Picture Service

Treaty of Madrid, signed in 1750, Spain formally recognized Portugal's claim to sovereignty over nearly all the territory that makes up modern Brazil.

Portuguese Rule

Portuguese rule of colonial Brazil contrasted markedly with Spanish colonial rule in much of Latin America. The ruling House of Bragança in Portugal allowed the governors of the Brazilian captaincies to exercise some independent judgment in local affairs—quite unlike Spain's highly centralized control of its New World colonies.

Brazil's gradual progress toward independence also made it different from the Spanish colonies. Most colonies broke from Spain only after protracted wars of independence. The chain of events that led to Brazil's independence was set in motion in 1807 when Napoleon Bonaparte invaded Portugal. Portugal's king, João VI, decided to move his entire court to Brazil until he or his heirs could regain the throne in Portugal. Napoleon eventually fell, and João VI returned to Portugal in 1821. He named his son, Dom Pedro, regent of Brazil and counseled the young

Courtesy of Museum of the American Indian, Heye Foundation

The handle of a pottery vessel made by the Indians of the lower Amazon Valley represents a human face.

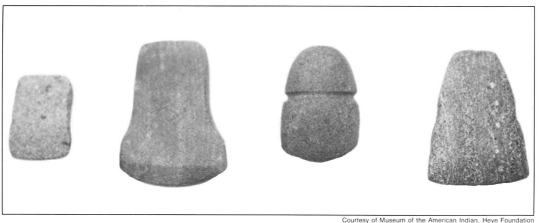

Courtesy of Museum of the American Indian, Heye Foundation

Axeheads such as these were used by some of the Indians of Brazil in their struggle to repel the Portuguese conquerors. Many Indians, however, accepted the Portuguese newcomers, and clashes were much less frequent than they were between the Spanish and Indians elsewhere in the Americas.

man, then in his early twenties, to declare Brazil independent when the time seemed appropriate.

That time came in the following year. The youthful regent declared Brazil's independence on September 7, 1822, in response to popular demands. A month later he was crowned Pedro I, Constitutional Emperor and Perpetual Defender of Brazil, an independent kingdom bound to Portugal by the family ties of king and emperor. The precise powers of the new emperor were defined in a constitution in 1825 that emphasized that he ruled with the consent of the governed.

Pedro I, strict by nature and upbringing, ruled harshly and was not particularly popular with the Brazilian people. Inspired by the French and North American revolutions and the wars of independence in Spanish South America, the colonists yearned to be in control of their own destiny, free from the dictates of Old World monarchs.

Faced with widespread discontent, Pedro I voluntarily gave up the Brazilian throne in 1831, after ruling for just nine years. Like his father, he bequeathed the throne to his son, Dom Pedro, who was not yet six years old. For nine years the Bra-

Photo by Nicole Ober, Visual Arts Unit, Organization of American States

The Ipiranga Monument in a suburban park near São Paulo commemorates Brazil's bid for independence in 1822. Beneath the monument is the Imperial Chapel where both Pedro I and his empress Leopoldina are buried.

Courtesy of Embassy of Brazil, Washington, D.C.

During the reign of Pedro II, the Indians of the Amazon—whose modern descendants still wear traditional tribal body paint—were accorded the emperor's respect. Pedro took the time to study Indian languages and frequently made the difficult journey into the jungles to meet with his Tupi and Guaraní subjects.

zilian Empire was ruled in his name by regents whose decisions, on the whole, reflected the will of the Brazilian people. In 1840 the 15-year-old prince was crowned emperor of Brazil—the first Brazilian-born head of state.

Pedro II

Pedro II ruled long—nearly 50 years—and productively. No other ruler of colonial Latin America was held in more popular affection while he ruled; few are more revered today than Brazil's Pedro II. A man of simple tastes and wide education, he was extremely popular with his subjects.

Intellectually curious, he sponsored the establishment of scientific and cultural societies, and he carried on a vigorous correspondence with many of the leading thinkers and literary figures of the day. He exchanged weather reports with the Arctic explorer Baron Nils Nordenskiöld and had a strong friendship with Professor Heinrich Schliemann, the archaeologist who discovered the ruins of the ancient Greek city of Troy. His fascination with Egyptology led him to study the Arabic and Persian languages and to examine Babylonian hieroglyphics (a writing system that uses pictures instead of letters). He also applied his language-learning skill during frequent visits to the Amazon Basin, where he acquired a basic conversational ability in the languages of the Tupi-Guaranian Indians.

During his long reign, Pedro II brought Brazil more prominently into international affairs. The continuity and stability he

Independent Picture Service

Two of Brazil's most colorful and best-loved leaders are commemorated in coins struck during their reigns. At top are the two sides of a coin featuring the bearded profile of Emperor Pedro II. Below that is a commemoration of the autocratic – but engaging – Getúlio Vargas, who was president from 1934 to 1946 and again from 1950 to 1954.

represented encouraged foreign investors to take an interest in developing some of Brazil's resources. Thus, the emperor's administration became a full partner in the acceleration of Brazil's industrial and commercial development. He personally promoted the construction of railroads and insisted that Brazil spend money to acquire telephones.

Historians fault Pedro II for giving in when the military urged Brazil to join Argentina and Uruguay in the War of the Triple Alliance against Paraguay in 1865. The allies won the war in 1870, but the struggle was costly. Popular dissatisfaction with the cost of this war was one factor in the eventual downfall of the monarchy, but also important was the issue of slavery.

At the emperor's urging, Brazil passed a law in 1851 abolishing the slave trade. Brazilians, however, could still own slaves, even if they could not import them. The total abolition of slavery was a controver-

sial idea, opposed by many economically powerful Brazilians. Pedro II's plan for escaping these wealthy proslavery lobbyists was to go on vacation in Europe and leave his daughter temporarily in charge. In his absence, his daughter actually passed the law abolishing slavery in 1888.

With many former slave owners against him and with discontent running high in the military, Pedro II was forced to give up the throne in 1889. During his reign, he had actually made careful preparations to leave. Pedro II had promoted the idea of Brazil's independence as a self-governing democratic republic, and he had thereby encouraged the political ideas that would one day force him to leave. When the day came for his rule to end, there was no bloodshed.

The First Republic: 1889–1930

On the departure of Pedro II, a Brazilian republic was officially proclaimed, and a new constitution became the law of the land in 1891. Unhappily, the transition was not entirely smooth. Regional rivalries, especially between the established plantation aristocracy of the north and the increasingly powerful industrialists of the south, troubled the nation and gave the military an excuse to intervene in politics.

Brazil's southerners won out in the national rivalry. Over the next 40 years, two states of the region, Minas Gerais and São Paulo, furnished all but two of Brazil's presidents. States and regions clashed with the central government in Rio de Janeiro over how much self-rule local governments should have. During this time, however, Brazil's railroads were improved, its harbors were modernized, and it grew as an international economic power.

Brazil's new commercial power was concentrated in a few industrial and financial centers in the south. Regional differences became more obvious, as did awareness of them. In the northeast, an area badly neglected by the southern politicians, pover-

Especially in southern Brazil, steel-making and other heavy industries took firm root during the nineteenth century. Since that time, however, the south has been equally dominant in Brazilian politics.

Courtesy of United Nations

Courtesy of Embassy of Brazil, Washington, D.C.

The *Correio do Povo* (Journal of the People) of Saturday, November 16, 1889, celebrates the proclamation of the Republic of Brazil and the end of monarchy with bold headlines: *Long Live the Brazilian Republic . . . The Army, The Navy . . . The Brazilian People!*

ty and disease were rampant. The old feudal aristocracy would never recover. The sons and daughters of the wealthy plantation owners spent their inheritance on luxurious living in Rio de Janeiro or Paris, leaving the fertile farmlands along the northeast coast unplanted while millions of poor blacks in the region suffered severe malnutrition.

When World War I broke out, the loyalties of Brazil's ruling class were divided. Most members of the upper class and much of the middle class sided with the United States and the Allies. Others were frankly pro-German, including Brazilians of German extraction in the south and some nationalistic military leaders. Brazil did not declare war on Germany until 1917, after repeated sinkings of Brazilian ships by German submarines. (It was the only South American nation to make such a declaration.)

Following the war, discontent and rebellion arose within Brazil's armed forces. The Revolt of the Lieutenants in 1922 was sparked by young officers who had been recruited among the lower middle class. They were motivated by concern for social justice and national reform, ideals that they did not feel their senior officers

shared. One reform-minded officer was a former army captain, Luiz Carlos Prestes, who organized a march to dramatize the need for national regeneration. Although many Brazilians favored his ideas, Prestes was exiled for his conduct and spent a good deal of time in Moscow. He returned an ardent Marxist-Leninist (one who follows the Communist ideas of Karl Marx and V. I. Lenin) and founded the Brazilian Communist party in 1934.

Getúlio Vargas

Brazilian politicians soon learned how to exploit fears of a Communist takeover, which were widespread among military and civilian leaders. Especially adept at this was Getúlio Vargas, governor of Rio Grande do Sul state, who ran for the presidency in 1930. When he was defeated at the polls, Vargas convinced the military to support him and seized power in October 1930.

Thus began the era of Getúlio Vargas, who dominated Brazilian politics for the next 20 years. When he assumed power, most Brazilians believed that at last they had a leader with whom they could identify. They thought Vargas would halt the

Courtesy of Embassy of Brazil, Washington, D.C.

This early photo captures a flight by Brazil's aviation pioneer, Alberto Santos-Dumont (1873–1932). Santos-Dumont is credited with having made the first heavier-than-air flight in France in 1906—a flight that lasted just eight seconds.

Courtesy of Colombo Cine Foto Produções Ltda.

An apartment block in Brasília reflects the modernistic tone of architecture throughout the city. Brasília was created in the 1950s as a new, centrally located capital that would be a symbol of national unity.

deepening unrest brought about by regionalism and by power-hungry politicians.

After being formally elected and installed as president in 1934, Vargas insisted that state loyalties must yield to national unity. A rewritten constitution, along with an intimidated congress, made it possible to remove barriers to interstate commerce, to declare a temporary halt on foreign loans, and to promote industry. Brazilian workers applauded as Vargas oversaw the enactment of the nation's first trade union. Further legislation gave women the right to vote and provided social security for Brazil's labor force. In 1932 a large-scale rebellion broke out in São Paulo, and the Vargas regime ended the violence after three months of fighting.

When he was threatened by conservative extremists, he proclaimed himself president for another term in November 1937. After dissolving an uncooperative congress, he took it upon himself to write a new constitution for what he called the *Estado Novo* (New State), which critics compared with the fascist model established earlier in Italy under Benito Mussolini. Civil liberties were curtailed. The press, radio stations, and even the nation's schools soon found themselves censored or given orders by a new governmental information agency.

What set Vargas apart from other South American dictators was his ability to make good use of able leaders, even those who had little sympathy for his methods. Public confidence in the government soared as Vargas appointed capable persons to posts as state governors, members of his cabinet, heads of the military forces, and ambassadors to foreign lands. Generous U.S. loans were used to launch a National Petroleum Council in 1938 and a National Steel Company in 1941, to extend rail-

roads, and to provide Brazilians with increased wages and better housing and medical care.

With the approach of World War II, Vargas had to maintain the support of pro-Axis Brazilian officers, many of German and Italian extraction, while not angering the United States. To display his personal neutrality, Vargas sent one son to the United States for schooling and another to Germany and Italy. Finally, on August 22, 1942, Brazil officially declared war on the Axis.

As the war's end drew near in early 1945, discontent with the Vargas dictatorship emerged. Military leaders forced Vargas to resign in 1945. After elections were held in 1946, a new government under Eurico Gaspar Dutra took control of Brazil under a new constitution.

The public became dissatisfied with the overspending, inflation, and political corruption that afflicted Brazil under the new administration. The nation's fragmented congress seemed unable or unwilling to cope with any of these problems. In 1950 Vargas was again elected to the presidency, but Vargas was no more able than Dutra had been to stem the tide of foreign debt. Wage earners were angered by the rampant inflation that eroded the value of their paychecks, and Vargas was charged with reckless handling of the national economy. The Vargas years ended in 1954 after gunmen hired by some of Vargas's friends wounded an outspoken newspaper editor and killed an army major. The military again demanded Vargas's resignation. A few hours after handing over the reins of government to his vice president on August 24, Vargas committed suicide.

Juscelino Kubitschek

A transitional government ruled for a short time, after which Juscelino Kubitschek de Oliveira was elected by the Brazilian people. He governed from 1956 to 1961. Undeterred by a worsening economic

Independent Picture Service

Juscelino Kubitschek delivers an address to Brazil's senate in 1963; Kubitschek became a senator after completing his term as president in 1961.

situation, Kubitschek went ahead to fulfill an old Brazilian dream—to build an entirely new capital city. Brasília was founded 600 miles northwest of Rio de Janeiro in a sparsely inhabited but centrally located area. When it finally became the capital in 1960, Brazilians enjoyed a burst of national confidence, a sense of accomplishment that lingers to this day.

Kubitschek had his detractors, including those who blamed rampant inflation on the cost of the new capital. His presidency ended peacefully in 1961 with the transfer of power to Jánio Quadros, a former governor of São Paulo state, who represented an opposition party. Kubitschek, who died in an automobile accident in 1976, was the last popularly elected Brazilian president to serve out a full term in office.

Military Rule

Jánio Quadros was elected in 1960. Honest and energetic, Quadros styled himself "the man with the broom," and he quickly used his broom in a determined campaign to root out governmental corruption. Even his own vice president, João Goulart—who had come in second in the balloting for the presidency—came under scrutiny.

Although the Brazilian legislature was dominated by Quadros's opponents, Quadros championed unpopular austerity measures. In addition, because Quadros believed Brazil needed to trade with all nations, he sought to reestablish relations with the Soviet Union and spoke warmly of Cuba's Communist leader, Fidel Castro.

Within six months of assuming the presidency, Quadros found himself hopelessly deadlocked with the congress and resigned the presidency on August 26, 1961. He was succeeded, after much political infighting, by Vice President Goulart—a man opposed by many Brazilians, especially the military, because he supported radical political ideas. Goulart's economic policies focused on basic reforms in land use and income distribution.

In spite of his intentions to reorganize the government to support these new policies, Goulart appointed unqualified persons to government positions. Furthermore, his financial measures aggravated an already overburdened economy. During his 31 months in office, the cost of living increased by about 300 percent and the value of the cruzeiro, Brazil's currency, dropped by 83 percent. In addition, the agrarian reform that Goulart had promised never occurred.

A military revolt deposed Goulart in April 1964. Strongly supported (some say planned) by the United States, the coup d'état was bloodless, but it marked the most drastic Brazilian rejection of civilian rule in this century. The next 20 years saw a succession of military men ruling Brazil on the basis of decrees called Institutional Acts. These military leaders shifted Bra-

zil's center of power even farther south. Most of them came from the country's southernmost state of Rio Grande do Sul. This state has long had Brazil's largest military establishment, as it borders the country's most likely potential foe, Argentina.

During 20 years of military leadership, opponents of the ruling regime were sent into exile or had their political rights suspended, and all news media were censored. The nation concentrated on crucial economic concerns. Brazil's success in the economic field—often referred to as an economic miracle—encouraged other South American countries to follow the Brazilian lead and to install long-term military dictatorships.

Throughout this lengthy period, no significant political activity was legal. Particularly in the state of São Paulo, dissent

Courtesy of Embassy of Brazil, London

João Goulart's presidency ended in 1964 when a military coup deposed the left-leaning leader. Popular support for the coup was strong, and Brazil continued to be ruled by the military until 1985.

was occasionally (and sometimes violently) expressed, but participants in these incidents were dealt with resolutely and brutally. Right-wing factions in Brazil used death squads—made up of off-duty police and soldiers—to assassinate political troublemakers, which was a deviation from the peaceful Brazilian norm.

Gradual Return to Democratic Rule

Under pressure from abroad and at home, successive military presidents began to liberalize the nation's political system. On November 15, 1982, Brazilians voted for state and municipal officials in the first elections in 17 years. Military candidates won fewer than 40 percent of the posts. Brazil's carefully controlled return to democracy took another step forward in January 1985, when an electoral committee, in which the military had a controlling percentage of the vote, chose Tancredo Neves, a civilian, to be president. Neves, however, died before he could take office, and his vice president, José Sarney, assumed the presidency. Sarney was elected president in his own right in 1986 and continues to pursue economic policies, such as limitations on imports, that are aimed to improve Brazil's ability to pay the interest on its foreign debts.

Government

Brazil has a three-part governmental system consisting of executive, legislative, and judicial branches. The country is also a federal republic, with 23 states, 3 territories, and the federal district of Brasília.

The elections of 1986 were the first in over 20 years in which Brazil's chief executive was elected by direct vote. The president and vice president serve six-year terms and may not be elected to consecutive terms of office.

The Brazilian legislature is a bicameral, or two-house, body made up of a 69-member senate and a 479-member chamber of deputies. The voters of each state select three senators for their area, who serve eight-year terms. The number of deputies, who are in office for four-year periods, varies according to population.

The supreme court heads the judicial branch, and its members are appointed by the president with the senate's approval. In addition, the states, the territories, and the federal district have their own lower courts.

The Congress building in Brasilia, the Brazilian capital, hosts both houses of the national legislature—the 69-member Senate and the 479-member Chamber of Deputies. (Photo by Mary L. Daniel)

Courtesy of Embassy of Brazil, Washington, D.C.

Colorfully dressed dancers samba through the streets of Rio de Janeiro. The samba, a swaying dance done to rhythmic, African-flavored music, became popular worldwide during the 1930s and 1940s. Samba's offspring, the bossa nova, became something of an international craze in the 1960s and influenced such 1980s musicians as Sade.

3) The People

With a 1987 population of 141.5 million, Brazil is the world's sixth most populous nation. Half of South America's people live in Brazil, and three-fourths of all Brazilians live in urban areas.

Race Relations

Brazil has a rich mixture of ethnic groups, the result of wave upon wave of immigration during four and one-half centuries. The Portuguese, in contrast to other European colonial powers of the past, showed a readiness to mingle with other races throughout their once far-flung empire. The union of whites, blacks, and Indians through formal or informal arrange-

ments has produced a wide spectrum of ethnic traits in Brazil.

In the 1980s Brazil's population was 55 percent white, 38 percent of mixed ancestry, and 6 percent black. The remainder was made up of Asians, predominantly of Japanese and Lebanese backgrounds, and of pure Indians, whose numbers have decreased to about 150,000. The white population, mostly of European descent, generally lives in southern Brazil. Blacks and people of mixed parentage tend to be found in coastal areas of the northeast. The Indians live mainly in the Amazon Basin.

Immigrants who came to Brazil after the colonial period—for example, the Ger-

33

Courtesy of Museum of the American Indian, Heye Foundation

An Indian youth of central Brazil fashions a headdress of twigs and feathers. Because their homeland is in the remote interior of the country, this young man's tribe has not intermarried with Europeans or blacks as much as have tribes that lived nearer to the coast.

mans, Italians, and French who settled southern Brazil—were less enthusiastic about racial mixing. Especially in the prosperous farming communities of Rio Grande do Sul, immigrants have maintained distinctly European cultural identities. Recently in one such community, Estela, not far from the state capital of Pôrto Alegre, 80 percent of the people still spoke German in the home.

Likewise, Brazilians of Japanese de-scent, who have become wealthy farmers and industrialists in São Paulo state and elsewhere, have chosen to maintain their racial and cultural heritage.

Racial prejudice continues to exist in Brazil, even though being black is not a serious obstacle to advancement and no stigma is attached to mixed marriage. Much of the lingering prejudice arises out of persistent economic inequality; blacks often hold the most menial jobs. Substan-

tial economic prejudice is also directed against nonwhites from the northeast, where much of Brazil's poverty is concentrated.

Language

Portuguese is the official language of Brazil. Brazilian Portuguese has an intonation different from that of its Old World counterpart—more musical, some might say. Brazilian idioms are also different from the idioms used in Portugal. Brazilian Portuguese has many words derived from African languages—which were spoken by blacks brought as slaves to the New World—and from Indian languages indigenous to Brazil. Indian languages survive today only among a few Indians in remote parts of the Amazon Basin.

Many middle- and upper-class Brazilians speak English, French, German, or Italian as a second language. While Portuguese and Spanish are distinct languages—not, in a strict sense, mutually intelligible— many words are similar in sound and spelling. Brazilians can generally understand Spanish if it is spoken slowly enough,

Courtesy of United Nations

The people of Catinga, a village in the lower São Francisco Valley, show characteristics of the three races predominant in Brazil's population. The man at far left and the little girl have European traits, the woman is of African ancestry, and the boy is an Indian.

Independent Picture Service

A farmer of the northeastern state of Pernambuco affectionately holds his son.

Courtesy of Jim Cron

São Paulo is one of Brazil's fastest-growing cities. Until the 1870s, the metropolis was sleepy and small, but it now stretches over more than 576 square miles.

although it is more difficult for Spanish speakers to understand Portuguese.

Southern Culture

Brazilians take pride in the survival of strong regional cultures, with prominent differences in attitudes toward work and living, music and art. Southern Brazil is cowboy country, with rodeos and barbecues (called *asados*), where meats of several varieties are cooked outdoors over banked beds of charcoal. The literature and music of southern Brazil—such as the novels of the great contemporary writer, Erico Veríssimo—often have strong, silent

main characters. *O gaucho têm fibra* ("the cowboy has backbone") is the explanation southerners give for their region's having produced so many Brazilian political and military leaders in the past half century.

The *Paulistas*

The people of São Paulo city and state, who call themselves *paulistas,* make up another distinct cultural group. The city's laborers and businesspersons are known as hard-driving, no-nonsense work addicts and are often considered humorless by lighter-hearted Brazilians.

São Paulo state is frequently caricatured

as a locomotive pulling the rest of Brazil's states like so many boxcars. The city and state exert leadership in national affairs. Next to the president, the governor of São Paulo state is Brazil's most powerful political figure. Brazilian businesspersons frequently look more to this state governor than to the central government for leadership on economic issues.

For such a huge city, São Paulo is amazingly well organized. Morning and evening rush hours are a modern miracle; carpooling is the norm, and subway and bus systems are efficient. The literature, art, and music of São Paulo reflect contemporary trends. Theatrical productions often stress the modern struggle to cope with the din and rush of urban living. The city's biennial art show, at which the most advanced painting and sculpture are exhibited, is internationally acclaimed.

The *Cariocas*

Because it was once Brazil's capital and because of its magnificent setting and beaches, Rio de Janeiro has long, in the view of foreigners, represented Brazilian culture. The people of Rio, who call themselves *cariocas*, are lively and imaginative—possessors of a rich heritage in all art forms. The city's most celebrated writer is the nineteenth-century novelist, playwright, and poet Joaquim Maria Machado de Assis. A mulatto, he made his way out of the slums, overcame epilepsy and a speech defect, and taught himself how to write. His works display indescribable gen-

Although Rio de Janeiro's Carnival is perhaps the most famous in Brazil, towns and cities throughout the nation celebrate, too. Brazilians dress in colorful costumes and dance in the streets until late at night.

Photo by Liba Taylor

37

tleness, haunting beauty, and irrepressible good humor.

Cariocas are particularly expressive and make living itself an art form by gracefully combining work and play. They enjoy a strong dose of zaniness and are known for eagerly awaiting the latest movies from France or Hollywood and the most recent Brazilian theatrical productions.

The city's pre-Lenten Carnival celebration is a gaudy display of fun that lasts for several days. In a burst of metropolitan fervor, neighborhoods from the poorest to the richest field groups of fancifully dressed people of all ages, who samba down the streets toward the center of the city. There, on the broad sweep of Avenida Getúlio Vargas, they shuffle and prance past reviewing stands where the city's elders, in mock solemnity, judge each group. There are prizes in many categories, such as song and dance, costume, and musical accomplishment.

Cariocas, speaking for Brazil as a whole, often sum up what makes the country work in a single word, *jeito*—the ability to accomplish something no matter the obstacles, to live life to the fullest at all ages and despite all infirmities. No word in the Brazilian language is more difficult to translate than *jeito*, though some scholars define it as the equivalent of Yankee ingenuity.

The Northeasterners

Northeast Brazil has a more sedate, though deeply inspiring, culture. Brazilians from other areas vacation in the northeast to visit historic sites and to heighten their appreciation of the nation's cultural roots. The two cities of Recife and Salvador, for example, are living repositories of Brazil's long past, particularly rich in architectural splendor and in Afro-Brazilian music, dance, and religion.

The evolution of this area is beautifully and exhaustively documented in the writings of Gilberto Freyre, a prolific contem-

Courtesy of Embassy of Brazil, Washington, D.C.

Brazilians follow international developments in the sciences and technology by reading professional journals from around the world. Brazil's adult literacy rate of 80 percent, however, is low in comparison to literacy rates in other economically powerful nations.

porary writer who is considered the father of modern Brazilian sociology. His best-known book, *The Masters and the Slaves*, chronicles how the northeast became a great melting pot, a place where the religious rites, music, and dance of blacks from Africa combined with those of the European colonists to form a distinctively Brazilian style of Catholicism.

Northeast Brazil has long been preeminent in the country's literature and art. A few of its most prominent writers are Castro Alves (1847–1871), the "poet of the slaves," whose statue overlooks the harbor of Salvador; Graciliano Ramos (1892–1953), whose sensitive accounts of the harshness of life in the northeastern backlands exposed the neglect of this region as a national scandal; and the contemporary

Independent Picture Service

The mammoth Maracanã Stadium in Rio de Janeiro is filled to capacity for an important soccer match. Brazilians have a passion for soccer, and some of the world's best players, notably Pelé, have come from Brazil.

Independent Picture Service

Resort cities in the cool Brazilian Highlands offer luxurious hotels. The Quitandinha Hotel at Petropolis is only an hour's drive from Rio de Janeiro.

Jorge Amado (born 1912), acclaimed globally for his novels set in his home state of Bahia.

Architecture and Music

The arts have flourished in Brazil since early colonial times, when European colonists constructed beautiful European-style baroque churches. Many of these churches still stand, and some have been restored to their original elegance. The greatest sculptor of the colonial period was Antônio Francisco Lisboa (1730–1814), whose magnificent religious figures in wood and soapstone grace the churches of the state of Minas Gerais.

Brazil has maintained its reputation for fine architecture in modern times. The city of São Paulo has high-rise buildings that are international trendsetters, famous for the graceful curves of their lines. Few architects are more acclaimed than Lúcio Costa and Oscar Niemeyer, who were the planners and architects of the new capital city of Brasília and of buildings elsewhere in the country.

39

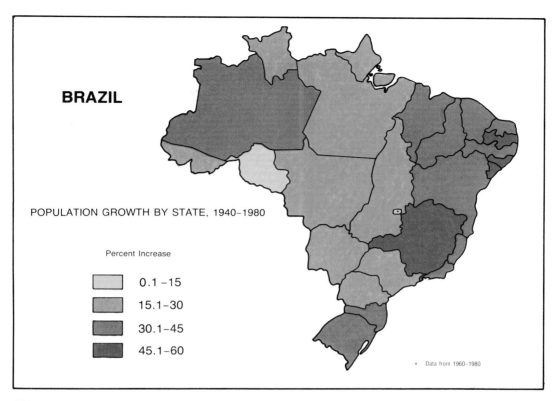

BRAZIL

POPULATION GROWTH BY STATE, 1940–1980

Percent Increase

0.1 –15

15.1–30

30.1–45

45.1–60

• Data from 1960–1980

This map shows how much larger the population of each Brazilian state was in 1980 compared to 1940. The figures represent the percentage of population increase over the 1940 population during the 40-year period. Data from *Tabulações Avançadas do Censo Demográfico IX Recenseamento Geral do Brasil, 1980.*

Although often of native origin, popular Brazilian music—such as the bossa nova, a complex, jazzlike form—has had widespread international influence. The compositions of songwriters like Antonio Carlos Jobim are worldwide favorites. In Brazil's concert halls, as in those around the world, the works of Brazil's most famous composer, Heitor Villa-Lobos, are frequently played. Drawing often on folk themes native to Brazil, Villa-Lobos wrote some 1,400 compositions, from symphonies to melodies inspired by folk tunes. Many of the latter, which he called *chôros* ("choruses"), evoke the mystery of Brazil's Amazonian jungles.

Health

Brazil's health statistics vary from region to region, as well as from income group to income group. A Brazilian born in 1987 could expect to live to the age of 65, which is about average for Latin America as a whole. Despite the nation's relative wealth, infant mortality in 1987 was 63 deaths in every 1,000 live births, a level that was higher than the Latin American average and quite high by standards of other industrialized nations. (The U.S. figure is 11 per 1,000.)

Many health problems can be traced to the slums, called *favelas*, that encircle Brazil's large cities. In some urban areas, 30 percent of the total population live in poorly constructed shacks that lack sewers and running water. Diseases spread easily under these conditions, and malnutrition is a common problem. Parents from the favelas who cannot find

jobs to support their children often abandon them. The homeless spend their youth begging and stealing to survive and sleeping in doorways at night.

A serious health problem—AIDS (acquired immune deficiency syndrome)—struck Brazil along with many other countries in the 1980s. The World Health Organization (WHO), which has assumed responsibility for worldwide AIDS research, reports that in April of 1987 almost 1,700 cases of the disease had been recorded in Brazil, mostly in urban areas. This figure is second only to the huge number of cases reported in the United States.

Education

Brazilian public education was restruc-
tured under military rule. Reform legislation that took effect in 1971 defined primary education as the first eight years of schooling and the secondary level as the next three to four years. By law, state and municipal governments are required to allocate at least 20 percent of their total budgets to education at these two levels.

The law also specifies a common nucleus of courses in Portuguese, Brazilian literature, history, social studies, mathematics, and science. Students opting for vocational training can choose among 130 specialized areas of training for jobs in industry, agriculture, education, and commerce. The last category has been the most popular, attracting one-third of all vocational students.

The public education system also includes undergraduate and graduate study.

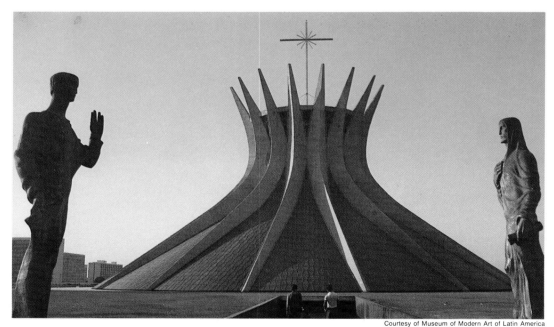

Courtesy of Museum of Modern Art of Latin America

The Cathedral of Brasília is a modern version of the crown of thorns worn by Jesus at his crucifixion. Brazilians, whose lively sense of humor plays on all subjects, joke that the architects had in mind the crown worn by the king of their Carnival celebration.

Brazil has approximately 900 institutions of higher learning, including 65 universities. Of that number, 44 are government-supported institutions that charge only a nominal tuition. The rest are privately run universities where the tuition may be high.

A tremendous surge in the number of students at Brazil's universities has led to expanded faculties in some fields and to the establishment of community colleges in less-urbanized areas, where the demand for education is high. The fastest-growing faculties are economics and business, as young Brazilians often aspire to careers in commerce. Competition for entry into medical and engineering schools is very stiff, as there are not nearly enough places to satisfy demand.

Statistics indicate that Brazil's system of education has worked reasonably well.

Nearly 80 percent of Brazil's adults are now classified as literate, as opposed to only 40 percent in 1940.

Religion

Most Brazilians are Roman Catholics, though in recent years Protestant sects have made some headway. Although some prelates are quite conservative and avoid involvement in politics, others take an activist approach, regularly speaking out from the pulpit on political issues and generally taking the side of the victims of social and economic injustice.

The Brazilian brand of Roman Catholicism incorporates a number of local cultural traits and is notable for its relaxed style. The African influences that have helped mold Brazilian culture as a whole

Courtesy of Inter-American Development Bank

Edson Ferreira shows students at a vocational school in Taguatinga how to convert a gasoline-burning engine into one that burns alcohol. Middle-level vocational schools are important in the government's plan to improve Brazilian education.

have also given a distinctive flavor to the Mass and other liturgies as celebrated by Brazilian Catholics.

Sports

Soccer is Brazil's national sport, and the nation fields teams that are among the best in the world. With dreams of playing on a professional team, youngsters begin kicking a soccer ball around an empty lot or a neighborhood playing field almost as soon as they can walk.

Under military rule, soccer stars replaced political leaders as national heroes. The most famous player of them all, Edson Arantes do Nascimento (called Pelé), is adulated nationally and has been a prime mover in popularizing the sport elsewhere in the world, including the United States.

Brazilians participate in many other sports—basketball, volleyball, and tennis, for example. Young Brazilians are conscious of the importance of fitness, and

Independent Picture Service

A member of Brazil's National Football Team (*left*) edges out an opponent in a race for the ball. Such international matches showcase Brazil's many world-class soccer players.

Courtesy of Inter-American Development Bank

This elegant restaurant in a four-star hotel in Vitória is also a school for apprentice waiters and cooks.

According to a recent Brazilian census, the nation's blacks make up 6 percent of the total population. They are concentrated in coastal cities of northeastern Brazil, where their ancestors were brought in as slaves to work on sugarcane plantations.

Courtesy of Museum of Modern Art of Latin America

jogging is popular, as are swimming and other water sports.

Food

By tradition, Brazilians like a moderate-sized breakfast. This consists of juice, fruit, and rolls with sliced cheese or ham for a filling. They take their breakfast coffee with an equal measure of hot milk and several spoonfuls of unrefined sugar.

Lunch is often the big meal of the day. In middle-class homes or restaurants, there will be rice, beans, vegetables, and a meat dish, frequently steak accompanied by manioc meal. (Manioc, which is plentiful in Brazil, is a starchy plant used in making

tapioca.) Poor people make do with rice, beans, and perhaps some tuna or a fillet of fish. The popular noontime beverages are soft drinks for children and beer for adults. Brazil produces soft drinks in a wide variety of tropical fruit flavors and excellent, reasonably priced beer.

The evening meal is often lighter, featuring salad, chicken or fish, and dessert, topped off with a demitasse of thick, black coffee.

There are, of course, many regional variations in diet. In the northeast, many favorite dishes are of African origin, and palm oil is used in preparing seafood. Southerners, living in cattle country, eat much more meat than the national

44

Courtesy of Inter-American Development Bank

Brazil entered the age of aviation early—its commercial aircraft began service in 1927—and Brazilians remain fond of air travel. Here, businesspersons board one of the many private jets that overfly the huge nation.

Courtesy of Museum of Modern Art of Latin America

Manabu Mabe is one of several outstanding Brazilian artists of Japanese descent. When he was young, Mabe practiced painting and calligraphy (elegant hand-lettering) and sold handicrafts from his home to support his art education.

Courtesy of Embassy of Brazil, Washington, D.C.

Many Brazilians are fair-haired and blue-eyed, particularly the Dutch-descended people of Recife in the northeastern state of Pernambuco.

In southern Brazil where there are many cattle ranches, a popular way of cooking meat is on skewers over a hot bed of coals.

Photo by Liba Taylor

46

average. Middle-class Brazilians of Rio de Janeiro or São Paulo use as many processed foods bought at supermarkets as do people in the United States.

On a night out, city-dwellers can choose from a broad array of menus; French, Italian, and Chinese restaurants are particularly popular. Fast-food restaurants have come to Brazil, a land where the hamburger has long been well known.

Brazil's national dish is the *feijoada*. This consists of beans, sausages, jerked beef, pork, cured meats, bacon, tongue, and the ear, foot, and tail of a pig. These are all cooked separately, then served on a tray with sliced oranges. Some of the meats and beans are combined in a crockery pot before they are ladled onto plates. Feijoada, a heavy meal, is reserved for festive occasions and is often followed by a nap.

Courtesy of VARIG Airlines

A modernistic sculpture by Maria Martins stands akimbo before the Alvorada Palace in Brasília.

Courtesy of United Nations

A resident of the Amazon Basin cuts jute on a riverbank. Only 5 percent of Brazil's people live in this vast region, which constitutes one-third of the nation's territory.

Courtesy of Embassy of Brazil, Washington, D.C.

The core of Brazil's first commercial reactor, Angra I, gleams greenishly just before the reactor's startup in 1982. The Westinghouse Corporation of the United States built Angra I, but Angra II (for which a site is being prepared) will be built by a team of West German and Brazilian experts.

Courtesy of Inter-American Development Bank

The thunder of cattle hooves is the sound of prosperity in Minas Gerais state, where sparsely settled territory has become ideal rangeland.

48

Courtesy of Inter-American Development Bank

With the help of a computer, a technician monitors pressure gauges at the water plant serving populous Rio de Janeiro. Brazil has a tradition of welcoming the latest technological advances.

4) The Economy

As Brazil moves toward the full restoration of democracy, the nation has much on which to build and much to do to make its economy work more fairly in the interest of all. Pressures long pent up under military rule have come to the surface, with both domestic and foreign businesspersons arguing for an economy as free as possible from government intervention.

Traditionally, Brazil has welcomed foreign investment. Foreign-owned multinational companies, many of which have Brazilian subsidiaries, are extremely active in lobbying for less government control. Foreign and Brazilian business leaders are hoping to alter the course set during 20 years of military rule, during which a great emphasis on national goals transferred much of Brazil's economic decision making from business to the government.

Modern Miracle

The economic strategy of Brazil's military leaders produced some remarkable results, characterized by some economists as a "modern miracle." In 1985, Brazil's economy grew at the rate of 8.3 percent—the highest figure for any major world econ-

omy. The country's tremendous strides forward were stimulated by Brazil's willingness under military rule to encourage the introduction of new technology.

In 1984, Brazil became co-owner with neighboring Paraguay of the world's largest single source of hydroelectric energy, a massive new power plant at Itaipú on their common frontier. The Itaipú power plant, built with funding and assistance from the World Bank, is an achievement of immense proportions and a major step toward Brazil's goal of eventually reducing its dependence on foreign sources of energy.

With assistance from the Westinghouse Corporation, Brazil entered the nuclear age in 1985 by throwing the switch at the first of a planned series of nuclear power plants. That same year, Brazil entered the space age by launching its first communications satellite aboard a French rocket at France's Kourou space facility in neighboring French Guiana. Internationally minded Brazil has dramatically increased its exports of manufactured goods abroad. Their value now exceeds that of such traditional commodity exports as coffee. Exploiting the global arms race, Brazil has become the fifth-ranked exporter of weapons of war—everything from tanks to fighter aircraft and warships.

Economic Disparity

Brazilians take pride in their country's emergence as South America's superpower—and a nation to be reckoned with on the world scene. The price of progress, however, has been a great deal of human misery and an ominously growing disparity between the nation's rich and poor.

Courtesy of Embassy of Brazil, Washington, D.C.

Construction crews near the completion of the gigantic Itaipú hydroelectric plant on the Brazil-Paraguay border, which will be the largest such plant in Latin America. Lacking significant petroleum resources, Brazil must derive power from other sources, such as its many rivers.

Slums known as *favelas* encircle most of Brazil's larger cities, which have woefully insufficient clean and affordable housing to accommodate the many emigrants from rural areas. The large cities of the northeast—Salvador, for example—are marred by particularly grim favelas, where people who fled rural poverty find a life as deprived as that which they have tried to escape. Decades of inattention from southern-bred national leaders have given the favelas a permanence belied by their rickety walls and makeshift avenues.

Courtesy of David Mangurian

Courtesy of United Nations

Agriculture in the semi-arid northeast is a precarious venture. When the rain falls, the soil shows its inherent fertility, but rain is all too infrequent and unpredictable.

Courtesy of United Nations

A government social worker visits families in a *favela* (slum) on the outskirts of Rio de Janeiro.

To a large extent, Brazil's military leadership simply ignored an entire generation of poor people, treating them as if they were beyond economic salvation.

Millions of Brazilians died prematurely of hunger and disease in the ghettos surrounding Brazil's major cities. Also, about one-quarter of Brazil's total population suffered because Brazil's military leaders, most of whom were southerners, did little to alleviate poverty in the northeast.

Many people in the northeastern city of Salvador, for example, lived among heaps of uncollected garbage, while the south prospered. By 1976, southern Brazil was the location of two-thirds of the nation's factories and 70 percent of its industrial jobs. The state of São Paulo alone, with less than a fifth of Brazil's people, ac-

counted for half of its blue-collar jobs and half of the production of such important export commodities as coffee, sugar, cotton, rice, and corn. Per capita income in São Paulo was more than twice the national average by 1970, while workers in large areas of the country earned only a fraction of the national average, despite the existence on paper of a minimum wage.

During the late 1970s and early 1980s, the disparity in earnings and production widened—so much that Brazil's military leaders, fearful of creating domestic upheaval, became increasingly reluctant even to make such figures public. To pay for massive public works and thus lay the basis for future economic growth, these leaders borrowed heavily from abroad, leaving their successors with a foreign

Independent Picture Service

To start new coffee plants, berries from the best trees (seven or eight years old) are planted in groups of eight in each corner of a specially prepared pit.

debt in excess of $100 billion. The mounting debt itself was a prime cause of the inflation that eroded the value of paychecks and hit hard among the poor, whose cruzeiros diminished in value during the briefest stay in their pockets.

The Transition to Civilian Rule

Brazil's new civilian leaders thus face the imposing task of realigning economic forces to promote social and economic justice, even as they seek to strengthen fledgling democratic institutions. This will probably require dismantling or liberalizing many of the federal and quasi-federal agencies that proliferated under military rule. By the 1980s, some 500 federally supported agencies had come into existence—in addition to traditional economic ministries, departments, and bureaus—and Brazil had established a cabinet-level post to oversee the reduction of bureaucracy.

South America's Megalopolis

Owing to local initiative as well as expenditures by successive military governments, Brazil has a strong economic base

Independent Picture Service

While the coffee seeds are germinating, each pit is covered with sticks set closely together. This method keeps the soil well aerated while retaining soil moisture and protecting the seedbed from strong sunlight, harsh wind, and chilling temperatures. *Coffea arabica*, the main species grown in the Americas, flourishes at higher altitudes.

Courtesy of Jim Cron

Sugar Loaf Mountain dwarfs the skyscraping apartment buildings of Copacabana, a suburb of Rio de Janeiro. Because of its beautiful scenery and location, this section of Rio is among the most densely populated parts of Brazil.

in the south. The process of urbanization is so advanced that there is almost uninterrupted settlement along the major highway from Rio de Janeiro to Pôrto Alegre. This mostly temperate zone of Brazil includes such commercially important cities as São Paulo, Curitiba, Florianópolis, and Pôrto Alegre—cities that are capitals of the prosperous farming and industrial states of São Paulo, Paraná, Santa Catarina, and Rio Grande do Sul.

This South American megalopolis extends to Montevideo in Uruguay and Buenos Aires in Argentina, farther south and west. A vital urban corridor, this continuous expanse of cities is comparable to what the coastal area between Boston and Miami, a similar distance, was about 25 years ago. Through the port cities along

the way—Rio de Janeiro, Santos, Florianópolis, and Pôrto Alegre—passes the bulk of Brazil's trade with the world, a trade in which Brazil enjoys a growing surplus.

To process the increasing flow of Brazil's agricultural exports and iron ore, Brazilian authorities constructed (at great expense) a new superport near Pôrto Alegre. To capitalize on its growing agricultural surplus, Brazil, like the United States during the first half of this century, invested heavily to develop worldwide markets for its harvests, particularly among the food-short, newly emerging nations of Africa. Brazil also deploys foreign service officers who are second to none in promoting their country's commercial interests.

To prepare for the future expansion of

the industrial and agricultural base of the south, Brazil has made a substantial investment in nuclear and hydroelectric power plants. The national government has also carefully nurtured a computer industry and created a network of scientific and technological research facilities and educational institutions.

Sharp increases in the cost of petroleum imports in the 1970s prompted federal agencies to develop a national program to promote the substitution of alcohol (made from sugarcane, of which Brazil has a plentiful supply) for gasoline as a fuel for vehicles. Cars that burn pure alcohol now constitute the fleets of some governmental agencies and are becoming more common as taxis in major cities. Gasohol, a combination of gasoline and alcohol, is now widely used in Brazil.

Brazilian authorities have encouraged the creation of companies operated jointly by the government and private interests to manage vital resources. Today, such entities manage the production and distribution of hydroelectric energy, the manufacture of petrochemicals, and a wide range of mining and processing operations. The Brazilian government is a partner in transportation systems, including airlines, and in the construction of hotels at places designated as priority targets in the development of tourism.

Northeastern Brazil

The problem area of the northeast still lags far behind the other regions of the country, although special tax incentives have encouraged Brazilian companies to

In contrast to Rio's dense settlement and extensive commercial development, Belém—the port of the Amazon—has a quieter, more colonial air.

Photo by Mary L. Daniel

THE TRANS-AMAZON HIGHWAY

BRAZIL

Courtesy of Embassy of Brazil, Washington, D.C.

The Trans-Amazon Highway, officially inaugurated in December 1973, links Brazil's easternmost and westernmost points on the southern edge of the Amazon Basin—a land distance of approximately 3,000 miles. The road has opened up an enormous area for settlement and has raised fears among ecologists who are concerned that the highway—long stretches of which are still very rough—may lead to the destruction of the world's largest surviving tropical rain-forest.

establish factories there and to construct tourist facilities in some of the coastal cities.

A special government agency, the Superintendency for the Development of the Northeast (SUDENE), was established in 1959, but its performance has been disappointing. Initially, SUDENE gener-ated such high hopes that it became a prime recipient of U.S. foreign aid. Today, its massive headquarters building in Recife looks starkly out-of-place. Locally, SUDENE is known as the "employment agency," a place where unemployed Brazil-ian white-collar workers go as a last re-sort to seek jobs with SUDENE's bloated

Courtesy of United Nations

Sisal—a plant used in rope making—is cut and bundled at a packing plant in the northeastern state of Pernambuco.

Courtesy of United Nations

Peanuts are another important crop in the northeast. Besides their edible beans, peanuts have leaves that are suitable for livestock forage and roots that restore nitrogen to the soil. Here workers separate peanuts from shells.

bureaucracy. The agency has failed to promote land reform, one of its primary objectives. To the contrary, larger and larger agribusinesses—successors to the plantations—have monopolized more and more of the northeast's production of crops.

Recently, Brazilian economists discovered that the most dramatic progress in the northeast has been achieved without governmental intervention. Economists coined a new word, *microenterprise*, for the very small northeastern businesses— generally operated in the home by a family or by a group of friends—that function without legal licenses and outside Brazil's established system of credit institutions and banks. Some 40,000 such enterprises do business in poor areas of Recife, producing a great variety of goods such as bread, pasta, shoes, clothing, building materials, mattresses, furniture, and craft items.

Microenterprises are vital to the neighborhoods in which they operate; traditional shops, markets, and manufacturers charge more for their goods and services than the poor of such areas can afford. Belatedly, the Brazilian government is coming to appreciate the enormous importance of microenterprises as employers and contributors to the national economy. Officials are taking steps to legalize them and provide them with access to credit.

The Amazon

In 1966, the Brazilian government created another regional agency, the Superintendency for the Development of the Amazon (SUDAM), to encourage development of potential farmland in this sparsely populated area. Following the construction of roads and villages, new settlers have moved into the Amazon Basin, especially

Courtesy of Embassy of Brazil, Washington, D.C.

Workers heading home from one of São Paulo's industrial plants use a simple, inexpensive mode of transportation – one that doesn't bog down in heavy traffic.

Courtesy of Inter-American Development Bank

The economy of this typical northeastern town is based on small-scale agriculture. The pace of life is slow and earnings are unpredictable.

Courtesy of World Bank

The fruit of African oil palms, source of one of the most widely used vegetable oils in the world, is gathered prior to being processed. Most of Brazil's oil palms are grown in the northeast.

Courtesy of World Bank

Welders work on a piling for a loading dock that will hold machinery to unload iron ore at the Sepetiba Bay terminal south of Rio de Janeiro.

Courtesy of World Bank

At a plant near Recife, inspectors test the quality of cotton yarn to be used in manufacturing Brazilian clothing. The state of Pernambuco produces much cotton and has helped Brazilian textile manufacturers establish a name for themselves as makers of clothing for global markets.

Courtesy of Inter-American Development Bank

Southern Brazil produces much of South America's beef. Paulo Pereira, an agricultural inspector, vaccinates cattle against hoof-and-mouth disease on a ranch near the town of Encruzilhada, near Pôrto Alegre in the state of Rio Grande do Sul.

where the lands are fertile in the sprawling state of Mato Grosso—which is about equal in size to Brazil's entire industrial south. By offering special tax incentives to industries willing to locate there and by improving the area's infrastructure, SUDAM has achieved considerable success. Foreign and domestic entrepreneurs have been eager to exploit mineral resources.

Some Brazilians have become millionaires by developing rich manganese and bauxite deposits near the mouth of the Amazon. One American entrepreneur, Daniel K. Ludwig, invested more than $1 billion over 25 years to develop the lumber and farming resources of nearly four million acres of Amazonian jungle at the confluence of the Amazon and Jari rivers west of Belém. Ludwig sold his enormous holdings in 1982 to Brazilian entrepreneurs eager to continue where he left off. His interests included an ingenious floating paper mill—which was constructed in Japan and towed across the ocean to Brazil—that can be moved along the Amazon from one logging site to another.

Courtesy of Inter-American Development Bank

Silvia Machado, a technician at a genetics lab in Brasília, grows cloned cassava tissues in disease-free nutrients. The hardy variety of cassava she obtains will be shipped worldwide.

Courtesy of Inter-American Development Bank

While visiting the old Dutch fort at Barra in the state of Salvador, a vacationer places an international telephone call. Communication from Brazil to nearly anywhere in the world is virtually instantaneous since Brazil placed its first telecommunications satellite in orbit in 1985.

A worker fine-tunes a valve at one of five petrochemical plants at the Camaçari petrochemical complex just north of the coastal city of Salvador.

Courtesy of Inter-American Development Bank

Photo by Meg and Don Malde Arnosti

The Itaipú hydroelectric plant—the largest in the world—is not far from the glorious splendor of Iguaçu Falls.

As Brazil moves to realize its centuries-old dream of developing the Amazon, national and international debate has focused on whether such development might permanently damage global ecosystems. Critics have already spoken out against the destruction of rain-forests along the route of the Trans-Amazon Highway, which provides the first land link between Brazil and Peru. Other criticism centers on fears that land-hungry peasants and developers are rushing in to stake their claims before anyone has found a way to build settlements that will not destroy the environment. A particularly heated debate focuses on the proposed use of toxic defoliants to clear huge sites for hydroelectric dams.

Still another cause for concern is the fate of Indians whose fragile forest cultures are threatened by the modern drive to construct new towns and roads. How Brazil finally copes with Amazonian development will have global implications because of the area's key position in the ecology of the planet.

Index

3 1799 00 168 5213

APR 1998

11/13-12

J
918.1
HAVERSTOCK
Brazil in pictures

168 5213

WEST ISLIP PUBLIC LIBRARY
3 Higbie Lane
West Islip, L.I., N.Y. 11795

REMOVED FROM
COLLECTION

D